The House of Tsutada

KINGSTON WESLEYAN
CHURCH LIBRARY

The House of Tsutada
The Little Man With a Big God

by Edna Johnson

The Wesley Press
Indianapolis, Indiana

Cover by: Lorelei Beth Ver Lee
Illustrations by: Tim Johnson

© Copyright 1988 by Wesley Press
All Rights Reserved
Published by Wesley Press
Printed in the United States of America
ISBN: 0-89827-061-8

Table of Contents

Foreword 7
Chapter 1 – But *You* Are a Tsutada! 9
Chapter 2 – John Makoto Tsutada 37
Chapter 3 – Mary Migiwa Tsutada 51
Chapter 4 – Joshua Tadashi Tsutada 57
Chapter 5 – The Twins: Grace Midorino
              Tsutada and Margaret
              Makiba Tsutada 67

Foreword

The stories in this book are true. The people you meet in the Tsutada clan are real people.

It would be impossible for anyone to remember exact words of conversations, even if they were said in one's hearing. Therefore, much imagination has gone into this writing.

This is not meant to be a biography of one man and his family. Rather, the stories are selected happenings from their lives. Some of the most interesting details of their lives remain untold.

When we get to heaven we will meet many, many people who will be there because one young man obeyed God.

This book is written with the hope that some child somewhere will be inspired to trust the same God David Tsutada trusted. If that happens, its purpose will have been accomplished.

I am indebted to my son, Tim Johnson, for the drawings in the book.

Chapter One
But *You* Are a Tsutada!

"That's going too far, Owen."

Young David Tsutada leaned over the ship's deck railing. By his side stood John Owen Gauntlett.

David listened to his new friend's words, "I know I am a child of God! I have faith in Jesus Christ. He forgives my sins."

David thought, Why do I wish to never see this man again? His strong belief appeals to me. But it disgusts me at the same time. He is no older than I am. HOW can he be so certain?

Just yesterday as David sat reading his Bible, a member of the ship's crew approached him.

"So you read that book, too! There is another young man aboard who is reading it nearly every time I see him. I will introduce you to him."

Thus the two met. David ventured this trip to London to study law at the university. Owen intended to enter a theological seminary in the land where his father was born.

David watched the moonbeams dance like jewels on the ever-moving water. The ship cut through the oncoming waves and left a furrow behind. Every minute

9

carried him farther and farther away from his Singapore home and family. His father, a Japanese dental surgeon, chose Singapore purposely to set up his practice. There are people from all over the world living there, especially from England. His children would learn from other countries.

"You can't teach me anything about God," David shot back to friend Owen. "I come from a very religious family. We are NOT heathen!"

As he said this, he imagined he could hear his father even now calling the family to morning prayers before leaving for his day in the dental office.

"At our house," David explained, "family prayers sometimes take hours, and Father is strict. All nine children have to sit perfectly still for prayers. We don't wiggle and shift for a more comfortable position. Each of us has to pray. We go by age. And we object strongly! But Father's word has to be obeyed. "My father would say to me, 'Yes, I *know* your friends do not do this, David. But remember: YOU ARE A TSUTADA!' "

David missed those daily prayers in his junior high years. He was sent to Japan for schooling. Learning the Japanese language is too difficult to do in a country outside Japan, even in Singapore. The writing is very hard to learn. Many of the written pictures can look almost exactly alike. One tiny line either added or left out makes a totally different word than you think at first glance.

So the very young David of junior high age had said good-bye to his family and gone to Japan. He spent all of his time studying the language and culture of his own people, the Japanese. All the while, he kept up with the required school work.

He learned to write more of these "picture words" than any of his friends, and wrote them more beautifully.

During university days in Japan, David worked for the Japanese representatives of the League of Nations. He received no pay for the work, but considered it patriotic service. They gave him an expensive watch as a "thank you" gift.

In that experience, he determined to study international law. Somewhere, sometime he could imagine gold letters on a door reading, "David Tsugio Tsutada, LL.D."

The big day of opportunity had finally arrived. He was actually aboard ship en route to England to begin the fulfillment of his dream.

As he listened to Owen's words, though, he wanted to run, or cover his ears.

As he turned to walk away, he called back, "I'll see you later," and went quickly to his cabin bunk.

I will read for myself the scriptures he quotes, he mused.

As he read alone, he came to John 6:47 NIV. Jesus was speaking these words: "I tell you the truth, he who believes has everlasting life." It did not read "maybe" or "shall have", but "has" life.

That fact silenced David. He did no more arguing with Owen. But he still did not have peace with God.

After a year of law study, a cable came from his Singapore home. With fear and trembling his fingers began to rip open the envelope. Was it good news? Was it bad news? He knew it had to be important news for him to get a cable that long distance from Singapore to London. He looked forward to letters, but that was all he expected.

As he unfolded the paper, he could scarcely believe what he was reading. His own dear mother had suffered a sudden serious illness and was quickly taken to heaven.

David's mind whirled. He was so far away. There

was no possibility of his getting to Singapore quickly. And even if he could, what could he do?

Suddenly he felt far away from home, from family . . . from God. He fell on his face to pray. But what could he say to God? He had not yet opened his heart to believe the words of Jesus he had read so many, many times.

He remembered again John 6:47. He knew his mother lives with Jesus forever. She had believed. And then he understood something else: because his mother believed Jesus died for her, she now lives. He also knew this: Jesus died for David Tsutada. He lifted his face and said, "Jesus, I believe You died for my sin. Right now I believe You to be *my* Lord and Savior."

In that very moment, David Tsutada became a new man.

After David became a Christian, he began to do all he could to help his student friends find Christ. As an active Christian leader, he set about publishing a paper in the Japanese language to share the good news of Jesus.

*****

We join David again in his last year of law study at the university. Only three months remained for him to attain his degree. Graduation day came closer and closer.

Because David was active in the religious life on campus, he was part of the planning of a big meeting in Speaker's Hall. A man named Asahina was to come from Japan for this special meeting.

David entered the hall at the appointed time and sat alone in a seat near the door. He saw his friend Owen across the room.

He sat and listened intently as the speaker read

Acts 1:8, "But you will receive power when the Holy Spirit comes on you; and you will be my witnesses in Jerusalem, and in all Judea and Samaria, and to the ends of the earth."

While he was still pondering the possibility of the power of the Holy Spirit in his own life, the speaker read "May God himself, the God of peace, sanctify you through and through. May your whole spirit, soul and body be kept blameless at the coming of our Lord Jesus Christ" (1 Thess. 5:23 NIV).

"Is there someone in this room who desires more than anything else that God by His Holy Spirit will control your entire life?" came the speaker's voice.

Yes, I am that person! David thought. But what would Owen say about this? For a moment he felt hesitant, and then with determination raised his hand.

"God bless that Japanese boy!" came the voice of the speaker again.

David felt a little embarrassed, and sneaked a glance across the room at friend Owen. To his amazement, Owen's hand was also raised!

The next day the English teachers invited those from Japan to tea time. The conversation went to the verses the speaker had read. Right there in that room both David Tsutada and Owen Gauntlett surrendered themselves completely to the control of the Holy Spirit in their lives. From then on they would never question whether to do the will of God, but only ask God to make His will known to them. That day changed their lives forever.

*****

After a few days, David was reading his Bible.
Jesus went through all the towns and villages, teaching in their synagogues, preaching the good

13

news of the kingdom and healing every disease and sickness. When he saw the crowds, he had compassion on them, because they were harassed and helpless, like sheep without a shepherd. Then he said to his disciples, "The harvest is plentiful but the workers are few. Ask the Lord of the harvest, therefore, to send out workers into his harvest field" (Matt. 9:35-38 NIV).

As David read those words, his heart was so heavy he could not sleep. He stayed on his knees praying until night came. He continued throughout the entire night praying.

Tumbling through his mind were the words of Acts, "Ye shall be my witnesses," and these from Matthew, "The workers are few."

Finally, when morning came, he knew what he must do.

As soon as he could in the morning, David made a trip to downtown London. He looked for the door indicating the place to send cablegrams.

He found a dark brown door and put his hand on the knob. Then he stopped and prayed, "Lord, am I doing the right thing?"

God spoke again to him as he listened. It was not a voice you can hear with your two ears. It was the Voice of God that is "heard" with the heart, not with ears.

"This is right, My child. Go ahead and do it."

Sure of himself, then, David opened the door. He marched with quick step over to the high counter. The very short David almost had to stand on tiptoes to look across the tall table. There sat a man wearing glasses, obviously there to help him.

These Britishers are so tall! Everything is too big! David mused.

"Sir, I want to send a cable to Singapore," he

spoke up clearly.

"Very well. Write your message on this paper."

At that moment David did not have to stop and think. He had already prayed. He knew the will of God. But his Father had sent him to London to study law. He must know what he would think.

Quickly he wrote,

GOD HAS CALLED ME TO PREACH THE GOSPEL STOP SHALL I PREACH OR PRACTICE LAW STOP TSUGIO

David went confidently back to the university. He felt great peace. He knew he had done the right thing.

He went to the library and opened the large law books and began studying for the next day's classes.

*****

In the morning he rose early to read the Bible and pray. It was not hard to do now. As a child, he only waited for the hour to be over. But now that he himself knew God, he loved to read His Word.

While he was praying, he heard a "Rap, rap, rap" at the door.

He opened it to find a uniformed man with a cablegram in his hand.

"Are you David T. Tsutada?" the man asked.

"Yes, I am."

"Cable for you, sir."

Quick as a flash, David tore open the envelope. He was surprised to find such a short message. In fact, it was just two words. That was all. But this is what it said:

OBEY GOD   STOP   FATHER

*****

"But Mr. Tsutada, you rank high in your class at the university. You have a bright future ahead of you. You surely must be upset about something to be saying what you are now telling me." The academic dean had a puzzled look on his face as he spoke.

David answered, "I am not upset about anything. You have been most gracious and kind to me here in London. Studying law is the thing I have wanted to do for a long time. And I have enjoyed it, even when it was not easy."

The dean broke in, "Then give me one good reason why you are saying now that you are dropping out! When spring comes, don't you want to be in that grand march wearing the cap and gown? Stop and think what you are saying!!" He raised his voice impatiently.

His words were falling on deaf ears, for David Tsutada was hearing another Voice (God's): "No one who puts his hand to the plow and looks back is fit for service in the kingdom of God." "Follow Me." "Don't be afraid." ". . . Ye shall be My witnesses. Ye shall be My witnesses. Ye shall be . . ."

Now David was ready to give his answer. "You see, sir, God has called me to preach the gospel. If I do indeed go ahead and graduate, it will always be in my mind. Preachers make very little money. They sometimes get along with less than they would like to have. If I have a license to practice law, I might be tempted to do that to have more money."

David stood up. "I wanted to be a diplomat for one nation – my beloved Japan. Jesus Christ is coming again to this world to reign – not over one nation only, but as King of Kings over all people. To be an ambassador for Him is better than for any one nation on earth.

"The King of Kings wants me to preach the gospel. I cannot stoop to being a lawyer."

David's own courage surprised even himself.

"I can see that your decision is made. If you ever change your mind, we will welcome you back," the dean meekly responded.

As the dean watched the small man with the giant mind and heart go out the door, he somehow knew he would never see him again.

David left that office and made his way to another business place. He marched boldly up to the desk. In a clear, rich voice he called out, "Give me a one-way ticket to Japan, please."

*****

The young man leaned over the deck railing. He watched the moonbeams make jewels on the water. He looked very much like the same David T. Tsutada who came on a ship to England. But that was four years ago. Now he was a new man. Same body. But a different spirit lived in him. Now he was on a mission.

As the ship neared Tokyo Bay, David prayed, "Lord, all I am and have is Yours. Every day tell me what to do. Show me how to do it. People in Japan need You. I love Japan. It is the land of my parents. I have many relatives there. Show me what to do . . . today, tomorrow, and every day of my life, and I will do it."

The ship jolted sharply and David knew the iron anchor had dropped to the sea floor. He climbed the metal stair steps to watch as they eased the ramp out to connect the ship and pier. His heart jumped as he caught sight of the land he loved.

Why is that large group of people gathered, and who are they? he thought. Suddenly he began to recognize who they were. Uncles, aunts, cousins and many relatives had come to Yokohama to welcome him.

He picked his way cautiously down the gangplank and the whole group came closer to meet him. He bowed low before them to show his respect and appreciation for their coming.

Then they shared the exciting news. A big celebration was to be held that very evening to welcome him to Japan. Many relatives would gather for the event.

Just then one of the group came to his side, to whom David bowed very, *very* low. (The more important a person is, or the more he is esteemed, the lower the bow must be. The very aged are held in high regard, and the head of the one bowing will probably touch the floor).

Who WAS this one David held in such high regard? It was none other than the Rev. Asahina, who had gone to England to minister and had led David Tsutada and Owen Gauntlett into full surrender of their lives to Jesus Christ (into the experience of sanctification).

This beloved man who had come to the pier to welcome him said, "David, you are here because you are called into the ministry. I have a meeting scheduled in the Osaka Church for you to speak tonight."

On hearing that, David turned to his relatives and declared, "Thank you all for your kindness in coming here, and for the plans you have made. However, I must preach the gospel tonight. Please enjoy the celebration. But I am sorry . . . I cannot come."

"What are you saying?" the puzzled relatives asked. "You are the honored guest. We insist that you come!"

"Please excuse me. This is what I must do!" he answered.

That night David spoke in Osaka on "The Judgment Seat of Christ." A man who heard the message

believed and gave his heart to Jesus.
David T. Tsutada's work in Japan had begun.

*****

David had studied in England, first in Cambridge and then in London University. But now he knew he must study the Bible to know it better. Even though he had grown up hearing it, there was much, much more to learn. With no salary, he must act on faith alone.

As soon as possible, David enrolled in a Bible college. He was happy in the study of God's Word. It was different from any other book. The difference was because it was God's Holy Word. God himself told men to write and told them what to say.

David had studied law. He found the books of law very interesting (Genesis to Deuteronomy). He enjoyed the history of Joshua through Esther. David Tsutada was a poet and wrote many songs, so he loved the books of Job to Lamentations, especially the Psalms, with their Jewish poetry. Isaiah to Malachi, books of prophecy, taught him many lessons.

Even as a Bible school student, he was out helping in churches. When he was talking to people who knew nothing about the Bible, he taught them from the Gospels of the New Testament (Matthew to John). He wanted to know more about the early church, just after Jesus went back to heaven. He found his answers in the book of Acts. From the letters to the Romans to 3 John he found reasons for his faith. He learned about the future in Revelation, the last book of the Bible.

Now sure of the reasons for his faith, David intended to spend his whole life saying, "The Bible is God's own Word to man. Every word of it is true. To believe it and do what it says is to have faith. We can belong to God through faith in Jesus Christ. Jesus died on the cross for our sins."

So David kept on studying. Often at night, and always on weekends, he went away from the school to preach the gospel. Sometimes there were only ten people who came to listen. Sometimes more. Sometimes less.

*****

"David, it is time for you to be getting married," said the school president as he stood facing him one day. "I have a girl in mind who would be a good wife for you.

"Nobuko is a capable young lady from an outstanding family. She comes from a pastor's home. Before her father entered the ministry, he had a successful export business in Osaka. When he felt God wanted him to preach the gospel, his wife objected, saying, 'No, I will *never* be a poor preacher's wife!' She loved the comfortable life his money afforded.

"But Nobuko's father became very ill and life left his body. The doctor said he had died. So the family called the men who take care of funerals.

"Nobuko's mother was heartbroken. She cried out to God, 'If you will give my husband back to me, I will do anything You want, O God!'

"The family could not believe what they were seeing! The man the doctor said was dead opened his eyes! They had read of miracles like that in the Bible. Here they were, seeing one with their own eyes!

"Her husband got well and she kept her promise to God. He preached the gospel for many years.

"That is the home from which Nobuko comes. And, David, the thing you will like most about her is her humble spirit. She serves people willingly. She is not proud."

"Whatever you say," David replied. He knew the teachers had prayed and thought a lot about it. They think about the families a boy and girl come from. Are the families something alike?

They think about how much education both the boy and girl have had. Would a certain girl be a help to a man because she also had Bible training? If she did not, nothing is said about letting those two marry.

If one family is very, very poor and the other very rich, they probably would not marry. Also, the health of both the boy and the girl (and their families as well) must be considered.

In America a young man chooses for himself the girl he wants to marry. It is best if the family thinks he has made a good choice. However, in Japan for many, many years the parents have made the marriage arrangements for their children. In the Bible colleges the president and the church leaders make the decisions if the boy and girl come from non-Christian homes. In modern Tokyo today, though, most non-Christians choose their mates for themselves.

David trusted those in authority over him. The parents agreed, and David and Nobuko agreed. So a wedding was planned.

This would not be a fancy wedding with a long white dress. David and his bride would not be the only bride and groom that day. There were three couples being married at one time!

After the wedding, David learned that the girl he had married loved sports. She was, in fact, a tennis champion, and was a good swimmer, too.

As they walked in the woods one day, Nobuko squealed with joy. "Oh, David, look! This beautiful little flower is low on the ground and almost hidden by other leaves. Isn't God good to let me see it today?"

The home David and Nobuko set up was very simple. They had only what they needed, and nothing more. One thing she very much wished for was lots of plants and growing things. Years later she had as many of them as she could.

When graduation from Bible school was over, the bride and groom went to an area of Tokyo to begin preaching. They wanted to start a church. It is hard to talk to people who have bowed before idols all their lives. The Japanese want a god they can see. David told them, "We cannot see the One true God in heaven with our eyes. And we cannot hear Him with our ears. But He hears us when we talk to Him. And He speaks to us through the Bible. His Holy Spirit tells us it is true."

One day David said to Nabuko, "We are going to have some special meetings to tell people about Christ. I will preach and lead the songs, and you play the little organ."

"David, I will pray for you, and I will pass out tracts and invite people to come into the meeting. But I am sorry . . . I cannot play the organ."

With those words Nobuko left the room and went by herself to talk to Jesus. At first she could not even pray. She felt so heavy in her heart. Tears began to sting her eyes.

Finally, while she was on her knees alone, she began to pray. "Lord, I know you wanted David to marry me. But what can I do? When other Bible school people come to help us, many of them can play the organ. But I can't. I am of little use in Your work!"

Then with the "ears" of her heart, Nobuko could "hear" Jesus talking to her. He was saying, "I made you the way you are because I want you that way. If you cry, and want to be someone else . . . then, you are right, I can't use you. But I have an important work for you to do. All I ask of you is that you give to Me all your heart. Give Me what you can do, and what you cannot do. I will lead you step by step."

Now with joy in her heart, Nobuko felt all clean inside. She went to the other room to tell David that she would do whatever was needed if God would help her do it. Most of all, she wanted to obey God.

David understood that. He too had promised to obey God. His wife had just made him very, very happy. For her to play the organ was not important to God. He had other work for her to do.

They continued to make plans for the meetings. They prepared little sheets of paper printed with the announcement of the meetings and the place and time.

"Come to hear the gospel! Hear singing. Hear someone tell you how he came to Christ. Hear David Tsutada teach you what the Bible says."

That is what was printed on the "hand bill." But there was one more thing at the bottom. Those words were, "Free admission."

Nobuko went out on the street with the other young people who had come to help. One of them saw a very drunk man leaning against a street light post. The drunk man watched them a while. Then they walked right over to where he stood. He reached out his hand to take the paper they offered him.

Just then a young boy came closer and began pulling on his arm.

"Daddy, come home! Mama wants you to come home! Don't fall down here on the street. Please! Mama sent me with you to bring you home. Remember?"

"Tha's right, son. Money's gone. Can't buy more drink. May as well go home," the man answered.

The man had already had so much to drink that he couldn't walk straight. As he stumbled and almost fell, the boy put his body close to his father's and pulled

his big arm around his own young shoulders.
The man's other hand took the paper, wadded it and stuffed it into his pocket.
As they neared the house, they smelled the rice cooking. They were thankful to have rice. When he used so much money to buy liquor, there was little left for food.
A full stomach made the man feel better. He sat on the floor and pushed back to lean against the wall. As he stuffed his hands into his pockets, he felt the wad of paper and pulled it out. He was still too drunk to make sense of it, but understood the words at the bottom.
" 'Free admission.' May as well go back," he muttered.
"Please stay here, Husband. Don't go out again tonight."
But his wife's words were not heard. He was already out the door.
As he picked his unsteady way and saw the lamp post, he remembered where he was standing when he was given the announcement paper. "Yes, this is the place," he spoke thickly.
He could hear singing inside. And then it stopped. He went up to the door and spied a short man standing in front talking to the people.
The still drunken man held out the paper and asked weakly, "Is this the place?"
Nobuko and her helpers were near the door. They knew he was still very drunk, but they did not ask him to go home. They readied a place for him to sit near the door. Then they handed a Bible to him, but he made no attempt to read it.
The speaker (Rev. Tsutada) was saying things the man had never in his life heard before. He couldn't understand. He talked about the healing of the leper,

as told in Mark, chapter one. Very few of the words stayed in the drunk man's mind. One word sounded like "Jesus", but it meant nothing to him.

He turned to the people who helped him and asked aloud, "What's going on here? What IS this?"

They whispered an answer in his ear.

After a while he again spoke out, "Who ARE these people?" Once again he was given quiet answers.

The meeting lasted very late. Then the speaker asked everyone to listen very carefully.

"Would you like to know Jesus? Do you want Him to change your life? Would you ask Him to heal you from sin? If you would, please raise your hand."

The man noticed some people put their hands up, so he put his hand up, too. He did not know what it was about, but if anything more was free, he wanted it.

The meeting ended and people began going home. A Christian man came and sat beside him. His hand held a book just like the one given the drunk when he came in. The helpful new friend opened the Book and read, "For God so loved the world that He gave His only begotten Son, that whosoever believeth in Him should not perish, but have everlasting life" (John 3:16). Then he kept talking about "Jesus."

Even in his stupor, the confused man volunteered, "Yes, I want to know Jesus."

He went home and told his wife, "They say they are having another meeting tomorrow morning at 5:30. I'm going."

After a night's sleep, he remembered more. He knew they called it a "prayer meeting."

"I know our religions have early meetings like that, but I didn't know these people who call themselves Christians do that," he said to his wife as he went out the door.

25

At that meeting there was so much life and joy that he promised himself he would attend every day. They also announced a Sunday meeting they called a "worship service". But the man owned a store which was open on Sunday. So he became faithful in attending the daily early morning prayer meetings.

So it was that a man even when he was drunk gave his heart to Jesus. As this book is being written, he is more than 80 years old. He has been a deacon in Tokyo Central Church for many years and won many people to Christ. The young son who went with him from bar to bar so that the father could find his way home gave his life to Christ and became a pastor and Bible school teacher. His children also entered the ministry. The former drunk's sister came to Jesus and married a pastor. Her son is a pastor and teacher. The grandchildren, as well, are preparing to be ministers.

This is the power of the gospel! God uses *people* to make himself known to other people.

*****

While David preached, Nobuko helped him in many, many ways. She invited people to the services, counseled many of the women and led them to Christ. She cooked lots of meals for people for Sunday noon so that they could stay all day and listen to the Bible teaching.

In time, God gave David and Nobuko five children: John Makoto, Mary Migiwa, Joshua Tadashi, and twin girls, Grace Midorino and Margaret Makiba.

Japanese people name their children very carefully. The Christians often take words from a Bible verse that have special meaning for them. For instance, David named the three girls from Psalm 23, "beside still waters" and "green" "pastures." The boys' names mean "truth" and "righteousness."

*****

The Japanese people faced hard times in those days. Japan, a small, crowded island country, and the United States, wide and rich in raw materials and natural resources, went to war. The men in power in the country of Japan felt they were being cut off from trade. They needed to buy and sell with the rest of the world. They were hard workers and loved their country.

On December 7, 1941 planes were sent to Hawaii to wipe out United States power there. The men who flew the planes knew they would die in the attack. They gave their lives willingly for the Emperor. They believed he was a god and it would be an honor to die for him.

The authorities required every Christian pastor to put up a Japanese flag in the front of his church. Christian services could still be held, but before the opening prayer, they must bow to the Emperor as they faced the direction of the palace. Only then could they proceed with the Christian worship service.

This posed a difficult problem for pastors. Some of them did just as they were told, saying, "We're just being patriotic."

David Tsutada and many other pastors felt it was wrong. They said. "Only God in heaven is divine. We worship Him alone."

Military officers often sent a spy to attend Christian meetings. If the pastor and people bowed to the Emperor, no one stopped their meeting together.

One Sunday morning David Tsutada rose to face his congregation. He observed that a newcomer sat among his people. He hoped he came to learn about Christ. In nearly every service someone comes in who has not heard the name of Jesus. When they hear, often they want to know more. As soon as the service is over, a Christian will go to them to help them understand.

The people too saw the man come in. No one knew him. Pastor Tsutada sat ready to preach, while one of his members came to the front to lead the people in reading the scriptures and singing, "Holy, Holy, Holy, Lord God Almighty." No one bowed to the Emperor.

Before this service began, the children in church school (Sunday school, it is called in America) sang in loud voices, "There is only One True God! Everybody, come quickly and believe Him."

The newcomer stood outside listening. When he entered, he heard, "Holy, Holy, Holy."

As the service came to a close, a Christian man turned to greet the stranger. He discovered the man had left during the last prayer.

A few days later a terrible thing happened!

You see, David Tsutada had his first Bible school in the building in which his family also lived. One early morning of that week he would soon be calling the family and students to morning prayers. The twin girls were the first of the children to wake up, because they were so young. One by one, all the children were gathered together with the students.

Suddenly someone was calling at the front entrance! David went to see who would be coming so early. There stood secret police, not uniformed, but wearing ordinary clothes.

They asked him, "Are you Tsutada Tsugio?" (The Japanese usually say the family name first, and the given name second. They would not be using his name "David" as it sounded too foreign.)

"Yes, I am," he replied. "Please come in. What can I do for you?"

They did not immediately come in, but announced,

"You are under arrest!"

David was wearing a cotton kimono, the usual at-home morning attire.

"May I first change my clothes?" he inquired.

At that, they pushed themselves in and began tearing up the house. They were looking through all his books. He had a large library, as he did a lot of reading. They threw many, many of his precious books into boxes to take with them to burn.

"These books are in English! That means you understand English. That proves that we cannot trust you. America is our enemy. Don't you know that?" they asked gruffly.

Then they yelled, "Tsutada, you do not honor the Emperor in your church! And you have English books! Whose side are you on, anyhow?"

Just because David Tsutada knew that God is higher than the Emperor did not mean he did not love his country. He loved Japan dearly.

David began to pray aloud, "Oh, Heavenly Father, take care of Nobuko, the five children and the students . . ."

The men pulled him away, treated him roughly and took him to jail.

David Tsutada's brother, also a pastor, was on a streetcar on his way home to his wife and family. Secret police got on the same car and took him off to jail. His wife waited at home for him to return, but he didn't come.

For two years about 130 men like David Tsutada and his brother were kept in prison. Seven of them died alone in their cells.

One time a month Nobuko was allowed to visit him. But each time she could see him only three to five minutes. She brought him what food she could.

Food was hard to get. Authorities told David's

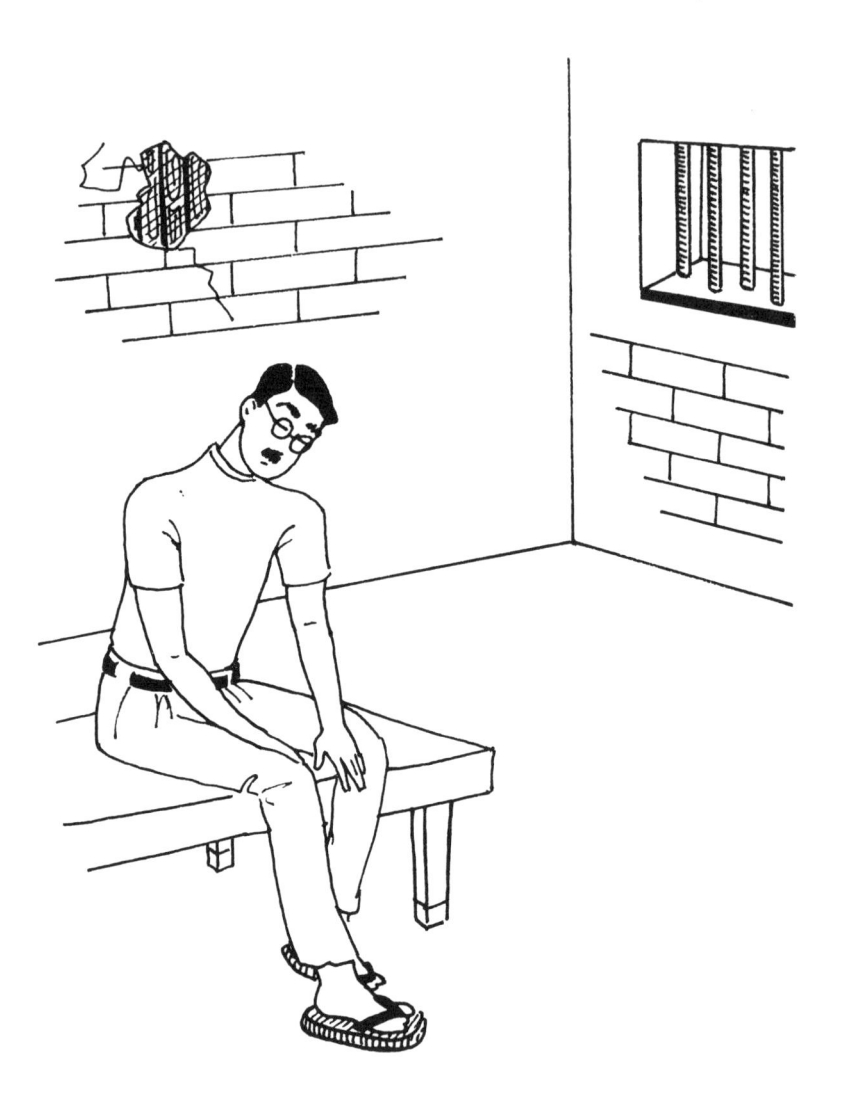

They treated him roughly and took him to jail.

church members they could not meet any longer. They also warned them not to have anything to do with Nobuko and her family. "Let them starve to death! That is their punishment!" they spoke harshly.

Some of them sneaked food to the family. They loved them so much, they risked their own lives to help them.

Nobuko made trips now and then to the country, trying to find food. Any growing green thing to keep them alive looked good.

She prepared food to take to the prison to David. Some days she waited many hours. Then an officer would come out and say, "No more visitors today. Try again next month."

With a heavy heart, she'd go back to her family. The twins cried with hunger. The three older children tried to comfort them.

The next month she went to the prison again. This time she was taken to David. He was lying down in his cell, too sick to come to the window. She fought back the tears as she saw his small body become more and more thin.

"David, how can you stand it?" she asked with deep pain.

"Nobuko, God is here. He is my strength. Every day I remember the name of Jesus, 'Immanuel', which means 'God with us.'

"He IS here, Wife! He is *here!* I will not lose my mind, because He is here! I talk to Him. He talks to me. He is telling me things I cannot tell you yet. But if I live, I will tell you." David's voice was strong with conviction, though faint.

"And He is with me, Husband. We have not starved. The children are too pale, but we are alive. Many people are dying. Tokyo has so little food." Her words spoke the grief of her heart.

31

At this, David gave her some advice. "Nobuko, listen to me. You must take the children and go to the country. Never forget, God will go with you. He has promised!"

"I suppose I must. But, David, we will pray every hour of every day for you to come home," she promised.

As she went out of the prison gates and walked home, every part of her body drooped with weariness. Her mind was no less tired. Yes, I must go to the country, she admitted.

The days went by slowly. David got weaker and weaker.

*****

One day before the end of the war, David was taken from his cell to stand trial in a lower court. Throughout the night he had been awake many hours talking to God.

He listened as he was pronounced guilty. But then he was released on probation.

David found a place with a friend to lay his weak body. When he could make his feet move at all, he appealed his case to a higher court.

It was that summer of 1945, while he was waiting for another hearing that the terrible war came to an end!

*****

As David Tsutada's body began to gain some strength, he began to contact his friends. He also made new friends.

Two ladies especially dear to him were a doctor and a nurse who had a hospital in Hiroshima. They were busy working there the day the atom bomb fell on that city. The hospital was destroyed. The nurse was crippled for the rest of her life. If you would go to Hiroshima or Nagasaki (where the second atom bomb was dropped) you would see some of the results of what happened. Buildings have been erected to display some of the actual clothing worn that day. Many other proofs of the damage done are shown there. A great number of people's scars from the severe burns remind those who see them of the awfulness of war.

The doctor and nurse went to a city in the Tokyo area. A sister of David Tsutada's and her husband, also a pastor, went to the same place at the war's end. (That man and wife were legally married while he was still a soldier in the Japanese army. For that wedding, the groom was absent!)

David and Nobuko, the doctor and nurse, the sister and her husband, and another couple ready to preach the gospel met together one day after the war. The eight of them knelt in the ashes of the spot where they were about to begin a new church.

David prayed, "God Almighty, You have delivered the eight of us from death. We are alive today and we thank You. Today we begin the new church for which You gave me a vision these past two years. We will call it 'Immanuel' because You, O God, *are with us*. Just as You were in the cell with me, You are with us here. We give ourselves to preaching and teaching the good news of Jesus Christ. As Your Word teaches the life of holiness, we will teach it. In the Name of Jesus, our all-powerful, soon-coming King we pray. Amen."

From the spot of those ashes of war came the Immanuel General Mission of Japan (IGM). By 1988, IGM members in all of the country numbered more than 10,000.

How many eights are there in 10,000? Do you

find that the people have become 1250 times what they began with?*

*****

By the year 1955, the Immanuel General Mission had sent three young men to America to study. One of them was John M. Tsutada, the first son of David T. Tsutada.

On this important day in June, 1955, son John was about to graduate from Houghton College, in Houghton, New York. (You will read more about John in Chapter 2.) He had the honor of being named to "Who's Who in American Colleges and Universities."

As the day of graduation came closer, John looked forward to it more and more. The special reason was that his father was coming from Japan to be the guest speaker.

The three young men got ready for his arrival. John had not seen any of his family for four years.

Finally the hour came. The Rev. David Tsutada arrived at Houghton College. First, Samuel went into the room where Mr. Tsutada was. He greeted him. Then Benjamin went to welcome him. (See Chapter Three.) Last of all, son John entered the room.

He bowed low before his father. He thought, Can this be my father? Four years ago he seemed young.

Today Japan is like a new country. Cities are modern. You are only reminded of the war as you visit Hiroshima and Nagasaki. You cannot go through the memorial buildings there and not weep.

Let's pray for men to learn love, and not hate. True love is only in Jesus Christ. Even today, less than 1% of the Japanese people know Jesus Christ.

Houghton College gives David Tsutada the honorary Doctor of Divinity degree

Here he is becoming gray-headed already!

For the graduation ceremonies the young men wore the caps and gowns to march in with the class. Attempting to keep step with the president, Dr. Stephen Paine, marched the little man with a big God, David Tsugio Tsutada.

Why was he there? Houghton College officials knew of the great work he had done in Japan. That was the reason they invited him to speak at the commencement exercises for the graduating class of 1955. But they had to build a special box to put on the floor for him to stand on. Otherwise, he would not have been able to see over the pulpit.

As he stepped up on the place prepared for him, he told that large crowd of people some of the story you have just read.

When he had finished, Dr. Paine put on David's shoulders the drape of honor, giving him the degree, Doctor of Divinity.

The title, "Doctor" David Tsutada, carried a greater honor than the degree that was nearly his so many years ago in London. He was being honored this day for his work for the King of Kings, the Lord Jesus Christ himself.

Doctor Tsutada was a small man with a big view of God!

Chapter Two
John Makoto Tsutada

A first son is important in Japan. He becomes "father" of all brothers and sisters he may have. It is a big job. Even after they are grown, he still helps them make decisions.

During the war, John had to be a strong big brother to the four younger children. He tried to be brave.

One day while his father was in prison, John woke up with a terrible pain in his side. His mother took him to see a doctor. He heard the doctor say, "John's appendix is about to burst. I must operate this very day."

"What will Mother do now?" he wondered. "She needs me."

John prayed for his mother and then knew that God would take care of her, Mary, Joshua, and the twins.

The doctor wearing a white coat came in and gave him something to make him sleepy. After several hours, he woke up and was told his appendix was gone.

While he was in the hospital, he had a big surprise! It was the best surprise he could wish for!

One day men he never saw before came into his room. With them was someone he *had* seen before, but didn't expect he could come in there to see him!

"Father!" John cried, and could hardly believe his eyes.

"Yes, my son. They felt kind today and let me come to see your face. It is only for ten minutes," he answered.

"Time to go!" the guards interrupted their conversation. Back to the prison cell they took him.

It was the first time Father had been allowed out of the prison.

*****

Schooling was difficult during war days. John was a good student and did his best.

After the war, the year John was a freshman at the university, Father said to him, "John, how would you like to go to America to college?"

"America! So far away? Who would I know there? No one. But if you say to do it, I will go," was his reply.

"I have decided to send Benjamin Chuichi Saoshiro with you. The two of you will go to Ben Lippen in Asheville, North Carolina. There you can get English practice before we decide where you should go for more study," his father explained.

*****

The morning dawned bright and clear and two excited boys took their suitcases to go with their families to the big ship in Yokohama harbor. Many friends came to see them off.

They walked up the gangplank of the cargo ship, then watched as the ramp was taken up. As the vessel moved slowly away from land, John and Ben waved their handkerchiefs to the family and friends on shore. They could tell which ones were Father and Mother Tsutada even after they were too far out in the bay to make out faces. Those two were waving their handkerchiefs – first up and down, and then back and forth – to form a cross.

"I think they mean we are doing this for Jesus' sake," John said to Ben.

*****

In California the two boys stayed overnight and then took a taxi to the train to go across America to North Carolina.

"John, did anyone say how many hours away North Carolina is?" Ben inquired.

"No. Didn't they tell you?" responded John.

So every time the train came to a stop, the two boys picked up their suitcases and stood by the door, waiting to hear the conductor say what city they were coming in to.

"Did that sound like Asheville?" John asked Ben.

"I don't think so," he answered, "but he talks so fast! And he sings it instead of saying it clearly."

They went back to their seats and sat down. A short while later they stopped again. Once more the two went to the door with suitcases in hand. They listened, and went back to their seats.

Japan is a small island country. Two boys so young could not imagine any country as big as the United States.

After four days of popping up and down, afraid they would miss their stop, two exhausted boys finally heard the welcome call, "Asheville! Asheville, North Carolina!"

The sleepy-eyed pair got off the train and greeted

the one who came to meet them. The first thing they asked for was a bed! They needed sleep!

*****

After four months in Ben Lippen, John and Ben were sent to Houghton College. There another boy joined them named Samuel Arai.

Before they came to the United States, John's father gave them a list of "Do's and Don'ts."

"While you are there," he advised, "speak only English. Even when you are together with no one else around, make yourself say what you need to say in English, or don't say it. That is the only way you will learn to speak well.

"Do *not* date American girls. You will see that the method of choosing a wife in that country is very different from ours. I want you to marry Japanese girls."*

Further, John's father gave them these three words, each beginning with the letter "P", to keep up their courage: "Remember this, boys, your parents will be far away, but you can always count on the PRESENCE of Jesus. When you need something, tell God about it. He will give you PROVISION. He will not always give you what you want, but what you need. And He will be your PROTECTION. No person can protect you all of the time, but God can, and will."

Japan today is changing. Many young people in the cities (other than those in Bible school preparing for ministry) choose whom they want to marry. In Bible school the choice is made for them by the church officials, but they can say "yes" or "no."

*****

The boys arrived at Houghton College ready to work hard at studying. As foreign students, they were not allowed to have off-campus employment, but John still says today, "That was good for our faith."

They found that many students worked at jobs on campus. So they visited the man in charge of student work. "Do you have something we could do?" requested John, who spoke for the three of them.

"Yes, we do have openings for you. Come back tomorrow and I will tell you what it is," came the answer.

In Japan, anything done in the kitchen is a woman's work. Today some men like to cook, but it is unusual.

As the boys returned to the office the following day, they heard these words of greeting: "I have just the job for you men! You may work in the kitchen scrubbing pots and pans."

Working with the other young people was more fun than John thought it would be.

"You are working so hard," he said to the cook one day. "May I do something to help you?"

"Yes, John, you may. I have all these potatoes to peel and I need to be doing the onions. The hands of the clock are going so fast, I am afraid I will not be ready with the meal when all the hungry students come in to eat. Your offer is welcome."

"I'll be glad to peel potatoes," John replied as he moved a stool up to work.

Just then he noticed a small group of people coming in the kitchen door. They were visiting the school and wanted to see the kitchen.

They talked to the cook . . . and talked . . . and talked . . . and talked.

John saw in her face that she was getting worried because she had no time to stop and talk. He suddenly had a bright idea. He went to the back room and got a little fan and hid it behind the big pan heaped high with sliced onions. He beamed the fan directly toward the visitors.

It worked! They began to wipe their eyes and started saying they must hurry on to see more of the campus!

*****

College days are for having fun. John made sure he had his share of good times. But he studied many hours, too. Often late into the night, his typewriter still clanged away. Roommates soon learned to go to sleep to its noise.

John and several other boys lived in the upstairs of Dr. Josephine Rickard's home. Everyone lovingly called her "Doctor Jo." She headed the English department at the college.

Dr. Jo noticed that having the boys upstairs was making her hot water bill go up and up and up. She learned that they liked to take baths with the water up to their necks.

So Dr. Jo made a rule. "Please measure five inches when you take a bath, boys. We must save water."

"We'll try," they promised.

Some of the American boys living there left for classes just about the time Dr. Jo came home at noon. She thought they had all left, but she could hear water running upstairs. One of them is still here taking a bath, she thought.

After some time she listened and the water was still running! "After all I have said about saving water, I cannot believe they are using so much!" she muttered, and stepped to the foot of the stairs to call, "Boys! Boys!" Each time she called, her voice became more loud and clear. "Boys! Boys!"

When there was no answer, she bounded up the stairs and no boys were there. She entered the open bathroom door, sure they had forgotten and left the water running.

There she found a dry tub. But a tape recorder was turned on full blast. One of the boys had recorded the sound of his bath water as it was running, and now he was playing it very loud . . . just to play a joke on her!

Dr. Jo was a good sport. She laughed and enjoyed the joke with them.

*****

One highlight of Houghton days came on Sunday mornings. Each week at 8:00 the boys from Japan went to the office of College Church Pastor Edward Angell for a time to pray together. They prayed for the services of the day, for the work in Japan, and for the people on their hearts. They kept prayer lists and when a prayer was answered, they wrote a "thank You" note to God beside it.

A closeness began between Pastor Angell and "his boys" that will never end.

Finally, the day of graduation came. You have read about that at the end of chapter one.

John's father, Dr. Tsutada, flew back to Japan after his visit. The three boys returned on a ship. As they came into Yokohama harbor, many of the same people who had told them good-bye four years before were there to welcome them back home.

One pastor at the pier cupped his hands to his mouth and called to the three young men who were standing at the ship's railing, "Do you still understand Japanese?"

"We do!" they answered in Japanese.

Even so, in the next few months they found that an English word often came first to their minds. Now they must do their thinking in the Japanese language.

John Tsutada came home from Houghton College to heavy duties. He was "in training" for leadership in the family. He began teaching in the Bible school at once. He also became a staff member of the Tokyo Central Church, where his father pastored.

Dr. Tsutada took John alone one day and said, "Son, I have prayed and asked God for a wife for you. The one He shows me is Yoshiko Saoshiro. And son, she is just like your mother!"

"Then, Father, that is good enough for me!" John loved his mother, and had her sense of humor, too. No matter how serious things were, there was always something to smile about.

"Son, another couple will be married in the same wedding with you. Benjamin Saoshiro's family and we have talked it over. You are to marry Ben's sister, Yoshiko (whom John later named Ruth). And Ben will marry your sister Mary Migiwa."

"That is very good," John answered.

That day in June two couples stood before Dr. David Tsutada to be wed. The brides wore lovely black suits, which they could later wear in the churches where they were to serve. The big white flower which each bride wore made the black suit even more beautiful. Each also carried a Bible. John and Ben donned tuxedos and clutched white gloves. As Dr. Tsutada joined their hands in marriage, it was like introducing each to the other. There would be plenty of time after the wedding to get acquainted.

John's mother, Nobuko, was the picture of dignity

in her black silk kimono, embroidered with the family crest. This gold seal (or badge) is passed from one generation to another and decorates the special kimono worn only for just such great occasions.

As each couple was pronounced man and wife, Mother Tsutada wiped tears from her cheeks. She was not sad. They were tears of joy that two of her children were now ready to work for Jesus.

From his father, John learned to love the beauty of the Japanese language. When Dr. Tsutada spoke, people listened. They called him a great orator. That means he had something important to say, and used words that were beautiful to hear.

John also learned from his father to use only that kind of language with his Tokyo congregation. Many university students and graduates attend there. But when he goes to the country to teach them the gospel, he uses simple words that are easy to understand. In Tokyo there are many universities. Farmers in the country do not often go to college.

In July of 1971 people all over Japan were shocked by sad news. Dr. David Tsutada, the one who began the Immanuel General Mission in 1945, and began the Bible Training College in 1949 (BTC), suffered a heart attack and was taken suddenly to heaven.

This brought John into three big jobs: (1) president of the Bible college, (2) pastor of Tokyo Central Church, and (3) he must now be the "father" of the whole Tsutada family. Besides this, he must continue translating books and doing many other things.

One day his deacons came to him saying, "Pastor, we have been meeting for ten years to pray for a new church building. It is time to begin to work now."

They knew of a Catholic hostel which was for sale. That four-story ferro-concrete building would take care of their needs until they could add a sanctuary.

"This is the very building we need. But where can we get $750,000 to buy it and build on?" John posed to them.

"We will pray for it," was their simple answer.

Every member of the board said, "Yes, this is the time." So they got down on their knees to pray. As they arose, one after another promised what money he could from his own savings. Some members of the church gave up land on which they were hoping to build a home for their old age.

The building and land were bought. Month after month miracles happened "just in time" to meet payment deadlines. Today a lovely church is their very own. It is a symbol of the faithfulness of God to help men of faith and action.

Many people have come to Christ through John's preaching. There are lots of stories that could be told of changed lives. If you walked into Tokyo Central Church today, one of the first things you would see in the entrance is an entire wall of pictures. These are of people who once were members of that church and are now preaching the gospel.

In 1984 Houghton College in New York, the school from which John graduated in 1955, gave the Rev. John Makoto Tsutada the same Doctor of Divinity (D.D.) degree conferred on his father 29 years before.

John and Ruth have eight children. At annual conference time there is a missionary service on Sunday afternoon. At its close, young people are invited to come to the front of the church to say, "Yes, I will go into full-time work for Jesus to make the gospel known."

"How many of your children went to the front today, Ruth?" a missionary friend asked her.

"Oh, all eight of them!" she responded, and seemed surprised that the question was even asked.

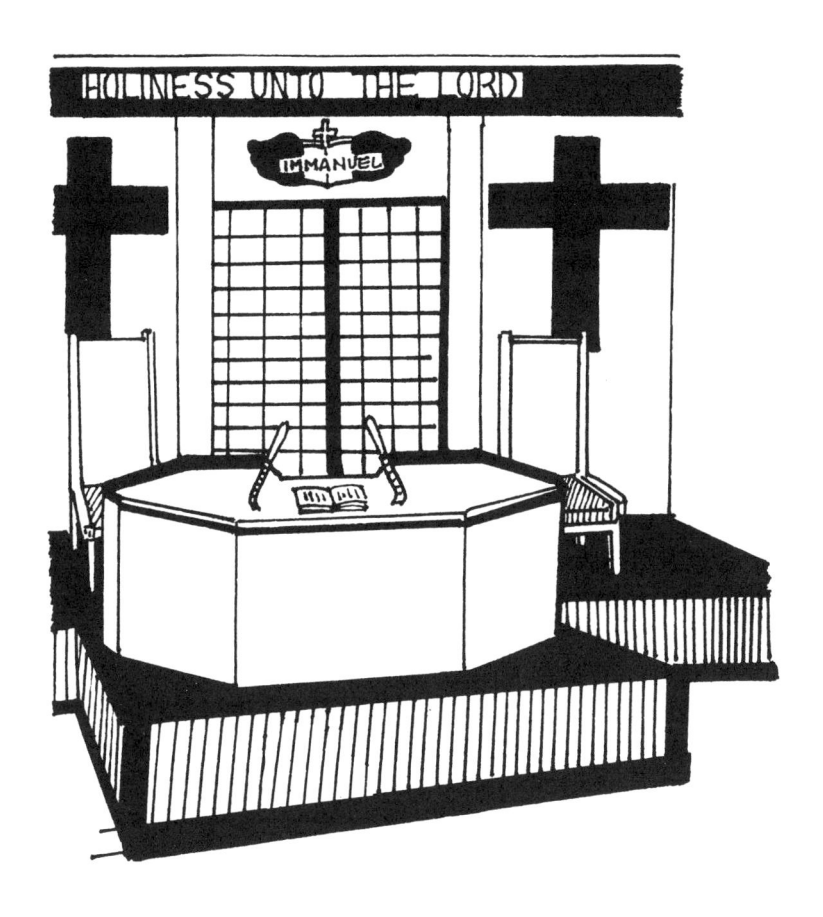

The Immanuel Tokyo Central Church, where the Rev. John M. Tsutada is pastor. The sliding doors behind the pulpit open to a baptistry.

One by one they are answering the call. David, the oldest, graduated from Oberlin College and the Immanuel Bible Training College. Then he went to America and earned a degree from Wesley Biblical Seminary in Jackson, Mississippi. After marrying the bride chosen by his father and the church, he at once became a member of the staff at Tokyo Central Church.

Sally, the oldest daughter, won high honors as she graduated with a degree in English from a Tokyo university. Next came four years at BTC, and now she has entered Asbury Theological Seminary.

John Mataki, the second son, completed a law degree in Tokyo and now is helping in "Immanuel Herald," a group producing cassettes of gospel messages. Many of the tapes are sermons of his grandfather's very own voice, Dr. David Tsugio Tsutada.

Jonathan Yasuki, third son, completed the course of study in a school of the Chinese language, graduating at the head of the class. Next he spent four years in BTC. Just before his graduation there, he wrote to his friend in America, Nathaniel Johnson, "Soon graduation will be over. In a few weeks I am to be married. But of course I do not yet know to whom."

For those of you reading this who are growing up in America, this system of wife choosing may seem very strange. But in many ways it is better than the free choice system. There have been no divorces among the pastors of the Immanuel Church. Perhaps they go into marriage thinking, "How can I best serve?" rather than, "Will I be happy?"

True happiness is in knowing the will of God and doing it.

When we who know Jonathan heard which girl was chosen for him, we felt great joy. She is the very one who can help him most. We can say the same for David's wife, and each of the marriages we have told you about.

Jonathan and his bride are waiting in Japan for permission from the Chinese government in Taiwan (Formosa) to go there as missionaries.

Benjamin, the fourth son, is a university graduate now in BTC for the four-year course there. Every BTC graduate enters some kind of Christian work. He decides that in his own mind before he enrolls.

Joshua, the fifth son, is now in the university. If you are guessing that he is to enter BTC next, you are probably right.

Anna, the second daughter, has entered St. Luke's medical training program and hopes to become a medical missionary.

Ruth Yorie, the third daughter, is in junior high school. She has already said "Yes" to whatever Jesus wants her to do.

*****

When Joshua Tadashi Tsutada was made president of BTC, John became chairman of the Immanuel Education Department. He also continues teaching in the Bible Training College.

Some nights John Tsutada sleeps only three hours, because he works late at his desk. And sometimes he works all night long without going to bed.

A missionary friend said to him, "John, you *must* take one day a week off. You cannot work seven days a week without rest."

What did John answer? "When there are eight days in a week, I will." You see, on Sunday he preaches, so that is not a day off.

Will you pray that many more Japanese young men and women will be saved and preach the gospel?

KINGSTON WESLEYAN
CHURCH LIBRARY

Chapter Three
Mary Migiwa Tsutada

Attending high school in Japan is a privilege, not a right. Entrance examinations are difficult. There are also exams to enter junior high school. And tests to go into primary school. And even entrance exams for kindergarten! If you get into a good kindergarten, you probably will be ready for the next school in line and have no problem, even on to the university. Kindergartens are not just "play times" in Japan. Young children learn much, and many schools require three years in kindergarten.

After high school, the hardest test of all is to go on to the university. High school seniors study late into the night to prepare themselves for college entrance exams.

Many fail. Then they feel they have brought shame to the family name. Some find it too hard to go on living.

David Tsugio Tsutada's first daughter, Mary Migiwa, was a very good student. She loved the beauty of the Japanese writing. She passed the tests to enter higher learning with top grades. The school from which she graduated is a famous one in Japan. The Emperor's

51

own daughter attended there.

After that training, Mary enrolled in BTC for her Bible training. Then when Benjamin Saoshiro came home from America, she became his bride, as you read in chapter two.

Mary was very shy. While she was still in high school, she came every week to the missionary's home for piano lessons. Then she had the evening meal with them before going to prayer meeting. Often when she came, she would say less than ten words the whole time.

God never changed her shy personality. Instead, He did a wonderful thing for her. He gave her boldness to win people to Jesus. It became her greatest joy.

Ben and Mary had three children, two boys and a girl.

One night Mary put her beautiful, healthy-looking second boy into his bed. She went again shortly to check on him. "Husband, come quickly! Something is terribly wrong!" she cried.

This precious gift God had given them had been suddenly taken to heaven to live forever with Jesus.

With heavy hearts, Ben and Mary continued their work. She turned her attention to the other two children.

At the same time Ben and Mary pastored one of the largest churches of IGM, he taught in the Bible school, served on many committees, and also became the chairman of IGM Foreign Missions Department.

For this reason, he often visits many countries around the world. One day he said to his wife, "Mary, we hope to have IGM missionaries in seven, and maybe eight countries shortly. I must make another trip to America, and this time you are to go with me," he said to her one day.

But Mary had news from the doctor that was hard

to tell her husband.

"Ben, the doctor says I have cancer," she finally admitted.

While they were still facing that fact, Mary got word that her dear mother was very, very sick.

From Christmas Day until March, Mary went often to the hospital to see her mother, Nobuko. Now they knew she had cancer. Mary saw that she was trying to say something. Mary stood close to her bed, but Nobuko's voice was too weak for her to hear the words. Finally, Nobuko reached for Mary's hand and began writing on it what she wanted to say.

"Now I understand better how much Christ suffered," Nobuko wrote. She had in her body pain too hard to bear. But an even greater pain was that some people she loved very much were not yet living Christian lives.

"God will take me home, Mary. But He WILL answer prayer, even later," she wrote on her palm.

In a very short time, Nobuko Tsutada died. She was the queen of David Tsugio Tsutada's home. Before he died, he showed friends her picture, and said, "I could never have done all the work that has been done without her!"

*****

"Mary, if you can stand it, I still think you should go to America with me before you go to heaven," Ben said to her one day. To his great surprise and delight, she agreed to go.

In America Ben and Mary attended the Christian Holiness Association meeting. Then they visited Japanese friends, some in Chicago and some in California. In each place there was much weeping. The tears were because they were so glad to see her, but also because they knew they would never again meet on this earth.

After their return home from America, Mary's pain increased. But every Sunday she went to the church services and spent time afterward leading women to Christ, one by one. Monday she went back to bed until the next Sunday morning.

Ben and Mary's daughter Gloria was one of the young people who gave her life to God to be used in telling people about Jesus. Today she is a student at the Immanuel Bible Training College (BTC).

Son Ken spent several years doing what he wanted to do instead of what God wanted him to do. But Mary kept praying. And Ben prayed. And many other people prayed.

One day the phone rang and Ben hurried to answer it. It was Ken.

"Father, a friend of mine is in real trouble. He needs money right away. I want you to pray," Ken begged him.

"I will do that, Son."

"I don't mean 'Do it later,'' Father. I mean, pray right now," Ken insisted.

With joy Ben prayed right into the telephone. It was the first real request for prayer Ken had made in a long, long time.

Meanwhile, Mary was getting weaker and weaker. As she lay in her hospital bed for the eighth time, she opened her eyes and was overjoyed to see Ken standing there.

"Ken, God is keeping me on earth until you give your heart to Him. It is time for you to do that," she told him.

"I know, Mother. That is why I have come," was his sincere reply.

In a simple prayer, Ken asked Jesus to come into

his heart and take control.

Very soon after that day the doctor said to the nurse, "Call Mary's family. They must all come."

Ben, and many family members went to the hospital room. They found Mary's body in great pain, but her face was beautiful because God was in the room with her.

Mary's two brothers and two sisters (the twins, Grace and Margaret) stood close to her bed and sang songs of Jesus' love, and of heaven. Then everyone in the room sang together! That music must have been something like we will all hear in heaven!

During her last days they asked her, "Would you like to have us play your favorite songs, on the tape recorder?"

"Yes, do," she answered.

While they were singing in the room or playing her favorite hymns, her spirit went to be with Jesus forever. She has no more pain. She is safe in the arms of Him who loved her.

Chapter Four
Joshua Tadashi Tsutada

Joshua is a "doer."

As a high school boy on his way home from school one day, he found a group of people standing close together by the vegetable store. They were looking up at a second floor window.

Joshua often went there on errands. But he did not really know them well.

"What's going on?" he asked.

"We think we smell gas, but the door is locked," they replied. Wasting no time, Joshua tore up the outside stairs and broke open the door. He found a man and his wife near death from the gas filling the room.

"O God, help me," Joshua prayed. He yanked open the windows and called to the people below, "Help me carry them out of here!"

He assisted in putting them into an ambulance, which took them to a hospital. They lived . . . because Joshua is a "doer," not a "watcher."

That spirit still lives in Joshua. He graduated from Rikkyo University, attended BTC for a time, and then went to India to study at Yeotmal Union Biblical Seminary.

Joshua loves the Indian people. After graduation, he stayed on as registrar (the one who keeps school records of students and their grades). On weekends he went out preaching.

He stayed in India 14 years, returning to Japan only for short furloughs. On one of those trips to Japan, he married Esther Hasegawa. Esther was his father's choice to be Joshua's wife.

Who is Esther?

She and her two sisters lived with their mother in Hiroshima when they were young. Her father was one who did not come home from the war. He gave his life in the service of the Emperor.

Esther's mother was sick at heart. And lonely. And it was hard to find food for three little girls and herself.

The day she got word of her husband's death, she had been called to the Hiroshima city office to receive the message. As she turned to leave, she walked slowly to the train station for the trip back to her home in the country. Her heart was so heavy, her whole body felt tired. Life was hopeless.

As she was walking, she thought of a plan that seemed the only way out. She decided that when the train was over the river, and not yet at full speed, she would gather her three little girls in her arms and jump from the train door into the river. The highest place on the bridge would be the best place to do it.

As she neared the spot, she took her three girls and went to the door of the train to get ready to jump.

At that second she "heard" a Voice, not with her ears, but with her heart. "Mutsuko!" (That is her name.)

"Lord, I hear You. But please forgive me for what I am about to do! There is no other way," she prayed.

"Where did you hear about Jesus, Mutsuko?" came the Voice again.

"From a missionary, Lord. You *will* forgive me,

won't You? I do love You, Jesus. But You would never ask me to do what I cannot do, would You? I *cannot* care for three little ones," was the only answer of her heart.

"And what promise did you make to Me when you were very young and first learned about Me?" God was still talking to her.

"I said I would be a missionary one day. But now You see how impossible that would be! My parents made me marry a man who was not a Christian. I hope he gave his heart to You before he died. He wrote me that he was reading his Bible.

"But now he is dead. What could I ever do now?" her tired heart kept arguing.

"Give me your three little girls. Let them become missionaries." It was clearly the Voice of God.

With tears streaming down her face, Mutsuko prayed, "Forgive me, Lord, for not trusting You. You may have my little girls. You may do with us whatever You wish," she promised.

She did not jump. She went back to her seat and rode to her country home, knowing that God was with her. He would supply all her needs.

Esther was the youngest of these little girls. Another one of the girls became a missionary to Jamaica and the oldest one spent two terms in Kenya, East Africa. Mutsuko kept her promise, and God kept His!

*****

Joshua and Esther and the three children God gave them had many good years in India. His love for the land and its people made the president of the school say to him, "Joshua, we need you to be teaching here at Yeotmal. Please think about getting more education so that you can come back to India to teach."

59

Joshua had already taught himself Greek, so that he could study the New Testament with some knowledge of the language in which it was written.

"I have been thinking of that also," answered Joshua.

At once he applied to Aberdeen University in Scotland to work on a master's degree under Dr. Howard Marshall, a man famous for his study of Greek and Hebrew, and especially for knowing Bible facts. Under his guidance, Joshua completed the work for the master's degree. And Dr. Marshall learned what Joshua believed it really meant to have the Holy Spirit living in and controlling a life.

"Esther, these two years in Scotland have been some of the happiest of our lives, haven't they?" he said. "But now it is time to go back to India."

But that was not to be. The government of India refused to allow them to come back. It is very difficult to enter India to do missionary work. One reason is that they have so many, many people of their own, the country is not able to have many foreigners come in.

That is the reason Joshua, Esther and the children returned to Japan. After a short time pastoring a church on the southern island of Kyushu, he went to BTC to help in the school. In time, President John M. Tsutada was made Chairman of Education and Joshua became the president.

In 1987 Wesley Biblical Seminary in Jackson, Mississippi honored him with a Doctor of Divinity degree.

A college president works long hours. So he is very busy. But Joshua sees the thousands of people living right around the school in big apartment buildings and wants them to know Jesus.

That is why Joshua began to hold meetings in the chapel of BTC for people in the community. His own three children help the Bible school students in the work of the church, especially in music. They also bring friends from their high school and elementary school to the services.

The church is growing and many people are coming to Jesus through the college church workers. Some of them are burning idols. One of them who did this was Mrs. Nezu.

Mrs. Nezu began to attend church. She had never heard anything like she heard there. The name "Jesus" was new to her. She watched the faces of people as they told how they came to know Him.

"Come have tea with us," they said to her after church was over one day. She asked many questions as they sipped tea.

One tea time she said to Pastor Tsutada, "I know now I need to let Jesus come into my life. But I can't for two more weeks."

"Two weeks?" he asked.

"Yes. I promised at the Buddhist temple to be faithful one year, and the year is not over for two weeks yet. That day I will pay what I owe there and come back," she explained.

Then she said, "A year ago 25 priests prayed over a charm and gave it to me. I was warned that if anything happened to the charm, or I did not keep my promise, terrible things will happen to my family.

"I have been coming here five months and bad things are happening. My son had a bike accident. I have bad dreams. Relatives are becoming strangely sick or have accidents.

"Now that I have chosen Christ, a fierce demon comes to me again and again. Pastor . . . I am AFRAID . . ."

Joshua said to her, "Don't wait two weeks, Mrs. Nezu. Jesus Christ has power over all demons."

61

He watched her face. It was bright with hope, and then dark again with fear.

"Go home and think about it," he told her.

The next day, Joshua's wife, Esther, phoned Mrs. Nezu. She heard her say, "I am ready to accept Christ today. I want to destroy every Buddhist charm I have, every prayer book, idol . . . EVERYTHING!"

That day Mrs. Nezu brought all of it in a box. She gave her life to Jesus and handed the box to Pastor Joshua.

The Bible school students made a fire in a metal barrel. As the pastor took it to the barrel, he repeated the name of Jesus to protect himself from the evil powers.

They all sang a hymn about Jesus and prayed. They thanked God for Mrs. Nezu's salvation. Then they put the box and everything in it into the fire.

A terrible odor came from the fire, different from any smell they had ever known.

Suddenly a high, fast flame shot out and around and around the barrel. The men had to jump back.

They continued to sing of Jesus and the odor vanished. The fire died down. All the idols were completely burned.

Mrs. Nezu knew then that there is power in saying the Name of Jesus, if you trust Him.*

*****

Joshua loves to tell one special memory he has of his father, Dr. David Tsutada.

"In 1956 the Bible school needed to be bigger.

---

*This story is taken from the article, "He Breaks the Power," by Dr. Barry Ross, Wesleyan World, November December 1987.

They put the box and everything in it in the fire.

Father signed a note promising to pay for land being sold next door.

"The day before the deadline, he still had no money with which to pay. The owner of the land called to remind him of the deadline.

"My father said, 'Tomorrow by the hour the bank closes, you will have your money.'

"The next day I had just come home from school and was playing outside. A man came in the gate and handed me a telegram.

"I ran inside with it and found Father coming from his prayer room. When I handed it to him, he didn't even open it right away. He just began dancing in circles, waving the telegram in the air. As he did that, he was shouting, 'Praise the Lord! Praise the Lord!'

"Only then did he open the envelope. It read, 'Sending you $2000.'

"My father got to the bank on time.

"But there was more to the miracle than that. The telegram had no address other than, 'David Tsutada, Tokyo, Japan.'

"We lived outside Tokyo, but God knew where we lived and got it to us on time!

"Later we heard the rest of the story. Mr. Ray, a man in lumber business in Canada had morning prayers every day before going to work. He had been a missionary in China, but could not go back because of poor health. For several days, the name 'David Tsutada' kept coming to his mind. He could not remember where he had heard the name. But he felt he should send $2000 to him in Tokyo, Japan. (Much later we learned that Mr. Ray had visited Japan once and asked a missionary whom he would suggest for him to send a gift of money. The missionary answered, 'David Tsutada.')

"But when he was feeling so strongly to send the

money, he knew no address. He went to wire the money, but the man in the office in Canada said, 'You can't do that. Tokyo is the largest city in the world. You need more address.'

"Mr. Ray insisted, and it was sent. God took care of the rest. We still do not know how."

Joshua can believe God because he saw faith at work in his father.*

---

*The content of the story of the $2000 is taken from the article, "Miracle Telegram," by Priscilla Probst, Call to Prayer, July August 1987.

The twins look very much alike.

Chapter Five
The Twins: Grace Midorino Tsutada and Margaret Makiba Tsutada

On the day the police came to take David T. Tsutada to prison for two years, he had to say good-bye to his wife, two sons, and three daughters. The babies were just three months old.

Food was hard to find and they were all hungry. But still the whole family managed.

Grace was born thirty minutes before Margaret. Now Margaret writes:

"I was the youngest child and was spoiled by my older sisters and brothers. I praise the Lord that He has changed me and trained me for giving out the gospel."

The twins look very much alike. They are both fun-loving. But they are serious when they need to be. People who know them very well say they can tell them apart from how they act, rather than how they look.

Sometimes they enjoy fooling people. But sometimes they wish they did not look so much alike.

Shortly after graduating from BTC, the twins took turns taking care of Mother and pastoring a church. A week or two at a time, one twin was at the church, and then the other one took her turn.

That made a problem. Someone came to talk to one of them, thinking she knew everything told her last week. Actually, that was the other twin. This one was hearing it for the first time.

Now it was the week for Grace to be in Tokyo. She came home from a meeting and knelt by the window of her upstairs room. She was looking at the moon as she talked to Jesus. (We do not always have to close our eyes to pray. If no one is there to take our attention and make us forget what we are saying to Jesus, that is especially true. He can read our thoughts, too, even if we do not say words aloud.)

Grace believed as she knelt there that God wanted her to be a missionary outside Japan.

"How *can* I, Jesus? I have a job to do right here in Japan," she argued.

"That is for ME to decide, not you," the answer came back to the "ears" of her heart.

"Anything You want me to do, Lord. I am ready," she responded.

Soon she talked to the Rev. Asahina, the president of the Immanuel Church. He listened carefully and finally said, "We'll send you to the Philippines to work in the Bible school with the Wesleyan church.

That is where she is today. She leads the choir and teaches other classes, too. Many students come to her home to talk to her. They know she will listen to them.

Grace loves the Filipinos. She does not know that she is changing at all. But other people see that she speaks and acts in a way that is a tiny bit different from most Japanese people.

One day when she was on furlough back in Japan, a foreign lady in the market inched her way close to Grace. She wanted to know how much a certain vegetable cost. So she asked Grace, "Excuse me. Do you speak Japanese?"

Grace went home laughing, "Have I become *that* different in so short a time that people do not know that I *am* Japanese?" she pondered.

*****

Grace's twin sister, Margaret, has interesting memories of childhood. She says, "When very young, my mother thought that in order to prepare for the work of the Lord, I should learn to play the organ. I did not like to practice the required 30 minutes a day. I would rather keep on playing games. My older sister had to practice more.

"Mother showed me the clock on the wall and said that when the hands got to a certain place, the 30 minutes would be up and I could stop. I soon learned that if you moved the hands forward, the time went faster. Actually, I practiced only 15 minutes, because I would practice a little and then move the clock hand forward. Mother was in the next room and did not notice the change."

She also says, "I have special memories of my father. He took note of the smallest needs. One time when I came home from the university he noticed my worn-out shoes and said to Mother, 'Take this girl down to the shoe store and get her some new shoes.'

"I wanted a tape recorder and asked Father about it. But I knew that my parents didn't have money for it. So I forgot about it. Sometime later Father came home carrying a little, inexpensive tape recorder. He called, "Maki! Maki!" as he entered the house.

"My happiness at that time was not only to receive the tape recorder, but that Father had remembered my wish. I was overjoyed.

"My father was very careful to teach us what was

proper to say in front of guests and how we should act. When we misbehaved, he told us by his actions.

"When we did not obey Mother, as a last resort she would take us to Father's room and he would use a switch on us. We thought it was the end of our lives!

"When I was in the third grade, I was in a new school in Urawa. It was a famous model school and very big. I was confused about which classroom to enter, for there were five buildings.

"I could have asked my family at home, but I was too independent to want to ask such a question. I was very proud and could not bring myself to ask for help.

"One day I could not find my classroom, so I walked around the school and played in the fields until it was noon. Then it was time for school to be out and I walked home.

"That went on for several days. But one day my teacher saw my mother at a vegetable shop and asked why I was not attending school. That was how she found it out. She gave me a lesson I could never forget.

"When Jesus changed me, there were many such things in my childhood for which I asked His forgiveness."

The day Margaret gave her heart completely to God, she did become a different person. After the university and BTC training, she did some pastoral work not far from Tokyo, as you have already read.

Then she was asked to go to a city far away from Tokyo to begin a church. She was sent to Beppu, a beautiful city with mountains around it. There are many hot springs there and people from all over Japan like to go there. The naturally hot water coming from the earth has minerals in it that are good for bathing. Even though sometimes it looks almost as brown as dark tea, it does not make clothes brown that are washed in it.

Margaret went to that city and knew no one there.

She began to tell people about Jesus' dying on the cross for our sins. She told them He rose from the dead so that we may live with Him. Margaret's teaching of the Bible was heard by first one, then two, three, four, and more and more. Another Bible woman came to help her. The two of them visited all the homes of the area.

Finally enough people believed the gospel and were baptized so that they could build a church. It is a white building, with beautiful hills around it. Usually on Sunday morning about 130 people came to hear her teach the Bible.

Margaret and her co-worker lived in rooms on the second floor of the church building. One night a frightening thing happened.

She thought she heard a noise and called, "Who's there?" But no answer came. As she watched, she called the police.

A man entered the room where she was . . . and then she saw it! . . . a knife in his hand!

Margaret cried to God in her heart for Him to help her, but no words came from her lips.

Just as the man drew back his arm and lunged toward her, the officers arrived, grabbed him and took him away.

God protected her!

Margaret made regular trips to a nearby island to have Bible classes in the home of a friend she had met there. This island is known for its devil-worship.

"Don't ever set foot on this island again!" the people told her.

But she kept on going. One person is trying to be a Christian there. Others will follow.

*****

March 29, 1988 was a happy day in Japan! You have learned in this book who the Rev. Benjamin Saoshiro is. He is a pastor, teacher, translator of songs and books from English to Japanese, and has charge of all the Japanese missionaries the Immanuel Church sends to other countries. On March 29 Miss Margaret Makiba Tsutada became his bride. She will work side by side with him to tell people about Jesus. We are happy with them!

The day she left the Beppu Church, 180 people came for the service. This is the place she was told that a Christian could not build a church. This is where God showed himself strong, because she believed Him.

Jesus said, "I will build my church, and the gates of hell will not overcome it" (Matthew 16:18).

*****

It was God who called the young Japanese law student, David T. Tsutada, in London, England.

And it is God who has chosen his children and children's children to bring many to Christ.

No one knows what God will do with a boy or girl who obeys Him. He has a perfect plan for YOUR life.

Do you belong to Jesus? Are you ready to obey Him? Do you read your Bible and pray? If you do, He will let you know what He wants you to do.

Read John 3:16 in your Bible and put your own name in the place of the word "whosoever". Read John 10:4. Then tell Him you will do whatever He tells you to do.